Basic Programming Essentials

Learn basic Batch, HTML, C, ...

appl...

Matthev

Description:

Learning basic programming skills and techniques is something everyone can and should do. You will write practical example programs throughout the book (that are free to run!) and explore the similarities between vastly different programming languages. At the completion, you will have a general understanding of programming and some new useful skills to brag about. We will cover Batch programming (free to run on Windows), basic HTML code (free to run everywhere), C programming (free to compile on Linux Ubuntu), and G and M code for CNC milling applications.

Table of Contents

PART 1 – BATCH Programming

Chapter 1: How to create, save, and run BATCH files

BATCH programs are run through the Windows command prompt. Anything you can write to the command prompt you can write in a BATCH program. You can write/create BATCH programs by creating a text document full of commands (that the command prompt will recognize) and opening/saving that text file as a ".bat" file. We will be using Notepad as our text editor. There are, however, many other free text editors you may choose to use. You can simply search the web and find some good ones. Some of these text editors make some parts of programming easier but since almost everyone has Notepad already, we will use that.

So first, open Notepad. We need some text before we can save/run a batch program. "ECHO" is a command used in BATCH to 'print out' something to the screen. So in a batch program, if you type "ECHO something", the command window will pop up and display "something" when the program is run. Type ***ECHO Hello, World!*** on the first line of your Notepad file. It is traditional when learning a new programming language to have your first program read "Hello, World!" (For the rest of this book, any text in italics and bold is text that should be written in the program)

Save the file to your desktop as "hello.bat" - this file will be saved as a batch program. Go to your desktop and your file should be there. Double click the icon, and watch your program run!

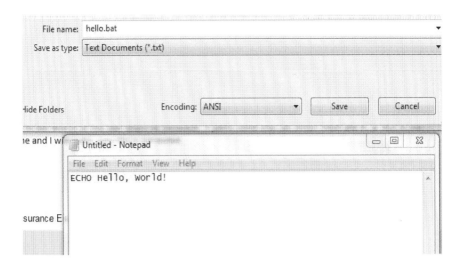

When you run your program, you will see the command window open and close very quickly. If you're lucky (or have a slow computer) you might even see the text, "Hello, World!" Let's fix this.

To edit your program, simply right click the desktop icon, select "EDIT", and Notepad will open the program's text. Type the word **PAUSE** under the ECHO text. Save your file, and double click the icon on the desktop. Your screen will stay up, and you can see the "Hello, World!", although it doesn't look pretty.

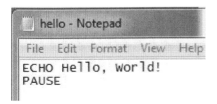

Chapter 2: Hello, world!

To make the results cleaner, go back into your program text by right clicking the icon and selecting EDIT again. Before the "Hello, World!" type **@ECHO OFF**. Save your file and run it again. A major part of programming in any language is making sure the output looks clean and organized - this will be stressed throughout the book. If the output is not organized, the user (the person running the program) may have a hard time reading and understanding the program.

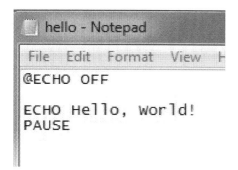

Now your program looks more organized. It is always good to have the first line of any BATCH program start with "@ECHO OFF" to make the program output look clean and easy to read. Now you may be dying to have a bigger command prompt window. You can change the size of the command prompt window easily by adding the following text after the "@ECHO OFF", **mode con: cols=160 lines=78**. You can change 160 and 78 to any numbers, you can try this. I will keep all my programs at 160 and 78 though.

Now, you may want to change the colors of your screen. You can easily change the background and text colors of the command prompt window in a batch file. To change the colors, we use the "color" command followed by two choices of color. The first color choice will be the background color, and the second will be the font color:

0–black 1=blue 2=green 3=aqua 4=red 5=purple 6=yellow /=white 8=gray 9=light blue A=light green B=light aqua C=light red D=light purple E=light yellow F=bright white

Add the text **color 47** to your file after the window size code, and run your program. Notice how the text is white and the background is red. Change the colors to whatever you want. Note that you can also change the font size by changing the properties of the command prompt window. Changing font size in a batch program is no easy task, so if you want bigger text, just right click the command prompt window and edit the properties.

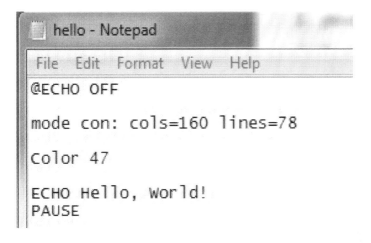

```
@ECHO OFF

mode con: cols=160 lines=78

color 47

ECHO Hello, world!
PAUSE
```

Now that we know how to change window size and colors and how to open, save, and run batch programs - we can really get started with learning batch programming. Our first lesson will be comment lines. Comment lines are extremely important in *every* programming language. From BATCH and HTML to C programming and G and M code for CNC machines, everyone should use comment lines.

In BATCH, a comment line is started with "REM". Anything that follows "REM" in the program will not be displayed in the command prompt window. Comment lines are there strictly for the use of anyone writing/editing the code. This is nice because it allows people (and yourself) to look back on your work and see why you did something. Say you created a BATCH file 25 years ago and some clumsy intern comes across the file. If the intern is good, they can open the file as a text file and read the comment lines to understand what the file is or how to edit it. Comment lines are very important - and even if you never plan to be a hardcore programmer, you should still use comment lines.

Go back to your program and add comment lines. Comment lines can be used to say why a program was created, when it was created, who it was created by, and can also explain why a certain command was used. The more comments the better! Add some comment lines and run the program again, and see how nothing has changed in the program output. If you would like to have additional space between the "Hello, World!" and the "Press any key to continue", go back into the program and type **ECHO.** between the "ECHO Hello, World!" and "PAUSE". Now run your program again. You can use "ECHO." anywhere you want to create spaces. I personally use it often, so you will continue to see it in the examples we do.

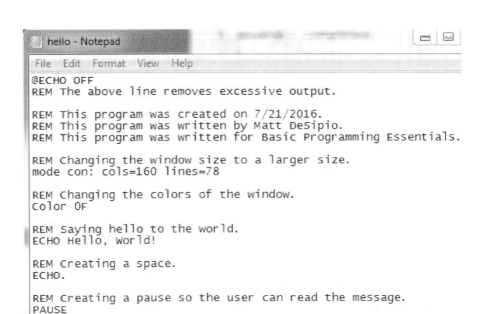

```
@ECHO OFF
REM The above line removes excessive output.

REM This program was created on 7/21/2016.
REM This program was written by Matt DeSipio.
REM This program was written for Basic Programming Essentials.

REM Changing the window size to a larger size.
mode con: cols=160 lines=78

REM Changing the colors of the window.
Color 0F

REM Saying hello to the world.
ECHO Hello, World!

REM Creating a space.
ECHO.

REM Creating a pause so the user can read the message.
PAUSE
```

```
Hello, World!

Press any key to continue . . .
```

Chapter 3: Variables

A variable is something we can assign a value to and use it later in our program. Variables can be extremely useful - in fact we will be using variables constantly. Variables are used in almost every (if not every) programming language that exists!

Open a new Notepad file and type your "@ECHO OFF" and any comments you want. Save your file as "variables.bat" and save it to the desktop. Do not forget to add pauses and spaces anywhere you may want them.

In our programs we will assign a value to a variable in three different ways. There are many other ways to do this, but since this is an introductory book, we will use these three methods.

The first way to assign a variable is to assign it directly. Let's say we really, *really* want to assign the variable "A" to a value of 3. This is done easily by adding the line **SET A=3** to the file. A is now equal to 3. This may seem pretty useless, but you will see the importance of variables soon.

The second way to assign a value to a variable is to ask a user for the value. Generally, the line of code used to do this follows the following template. "SET /P variable = question". So let's say we want the user to assign a value to the letter "B". To do this, we add the following line of code to our file **SET /P B=Please enter your value of B here, then press ENTER:** . Note the additional space after the colon. This is good practice because it makes the user entry much easier to read in the output. Try it without the space and then try it again with the space. What do you think looks better?

Obviously, the second method seems a little more useful than the first. In our file, "A" is equal to 3 and "B" is equal to whatever the user enters.

The third method we will cover of assigning variables will be through mathematics. To do this, add the line "SET /A variable = math goes here". Let's make a variable "RESULT" (variables can be any word/letter you want for the most part) and assign it to the value of the subtraction of 2 from 5.

Add the line **SET /A RESULT= 5 - 2** to your file. RESULT is now equal to 3.

This is good and all, but none of these values will actually be displayed on the screen for the user to see. To display a variable, you must surround it with "%"'s (percent signs). In BATCH, if you were to type *ECHO A*, the output would be "A". However, if you were to type *ECHO %A%*, the output would be "3".

Add this line of code under everything else, followed by a pause: **ECHO A is equal to %A%, B is equal to %B%, and RESULT is equal to %RESULT%**. Save and run your program. Try the program without the "%"'s if you are curious.

```
C:\WINDOWS\system32\cmd.exe
Please enter your value of B here, then press ENTER: 5
A is equal to 3, B is equal to 5, and RESULT is equal to 3
Press any key to continue . . .
```

We have successfully printed variables to the screen, but how is this useful? Well let's ask the user to assign a value to two variables for us. Let's add the following lines of code to our file: **SET /P C=Please enter your first number here:** and **SET /P D=Please enter your second number here:** . Again, note the spaces after the colons. Now that we have values assigned to C and D, let's multiply them and make the result a variable "solution".

SET /A solution= %C%*%D%. Make sure to surround the C and D with "%"'s or else the program will not work. ALWAYS SURROUND VARIABLES IN PERCENT SIGNS. Let's add the following line of text, **ECHO the multiplication of %C% and %D% is %solution%**.

Make sure to add pauses/spaces anywhere you wish. Congratulations, you have just created a multiplication calculator. Maybe this isn't the most groundbreaking program ever written, but it is a useful application of some very simple batch programming.

```
@ECHO OFF
REM The above line removes excessive output.

REM This program was created on 7/21/2016.
REM This program was written by Matt DeSipio.
REM This program was written for Basic Programming Essentials.

REM Changing the window size to a larger size.
mode con: cols=160 lines=78

REM Changing the colors of the window.
Color OF

REM Setting A equal to 3.
SET A=3

REM Setting B equal to a user inputted response.
SET /P B=Please enter your value of B here, then press ENTER:

REM Setting RESULT.
SET /A RESULT = 5 - 2

REM Printing Results.
ECHO.
ECHO A is equal to %A%, B is equal to %B%, and RESULT is equal to

REM Adding a pause.
ECHO.
PAUSE
ECHO.

REM Setting C equal to a user inputted response.
SET /P C=Please enter your value of C here, then press ENTER:
ECHO.

REM Setting D equal to a user inputted response.
SET /P D=Please enter your value of D here, then press ENTER:
ECHO.

REM Finding the solution.
SET /a solution= %C%*%D%

REM Printing results.
ECHO The multiplication of %C% and %D% is %solution%

REM Creating a final pause.
ECHO.
PAUSE
```

```
C:\WINDOWS\system32\cmd.exe

Please enter your value of B here, then press ENTER: 3
A is equal to 3, B is equal to 3, and RESULT is equal to 3
Press any key to continue . . .
Please enter your value of C here, then press ENTER: 5
Please enter your value of D here, then press ENTER: 2
The multiplication of 5 and 2 is 10
Press any key to continue . . .
```

Note that there is a lot of different math you can do in BATCH, but for our purposes just know "+" is addition, "-" is subtraction, "/" is division, and "*" is multiplication. Be cautious of declaring variables inside logic statements and loops.

Chapter 4: IF statements

From chapter 2 to chapter 3, we took a giant leap. Let's take one more. IF statements are vital to programming and learning the logic behind them is a great and useful skill (they are also relatively easy). While many languages have different syntax, the basic logic behind the IF statement is always the same.

An IF statement is set up something like "IF X related to Y (Do this)". The program will only go inside of the IF statement (do the commands in parenthesis) if the statement before it is true (If X related to Y).

So, if you have X = 4, and Y = 4, and an IF statement that starts "IF X EQU y (command)", the command in parenthesis following the statement will be done. (EQU means "is equal to")

If the program reads...

```
menu - Notepad
File  Edit  Format  View  Help
@ECHO OFF
REM The above line removes excessive output.

REM This program was created on 7/21/2016.
REM This program was written by Matt DeSipio.
REM This program was written for Basic Programming Essentials.

REM Changing the window size to a larger size.
mode con: cols=160 lines=78

REM Changing the colors of the window.
Color 0F

REM Setting X equal to 4.
SET X=4
REM Setting Y equal to 4.
SET Y=4

IF %X% EQU %Y% (
        ECHO X and Y are equal!
)

REM Creating a pause.
ECHO.
PAUSE
```

The command window will display "X and Y are equal!" Note where X and Y are surrounded in "%"'s.

In addition to EQU, you can also use NEQ (is not equal to), GEQ (is greater than or equal to), and LEQ (is less than or equal to). We also see the indent inside the IF statement. When you start writing some long and complex programs, organizing your code is key. If your code doesn't run properly, you have to troubleshoot and troubleshooting is much easier when your code is organized and neat. Generally, you can indent however you want (some of those text editors even indent automatically), but it is good practice to indent inside statements/loops in *every* programming language.

IF statements are relatively easy to understand, so let's start creating our example file. Open Notepad, add "@ECHO OFF", comments, and spaces; and save the file as "menu.bat". We will create a menu in which the user can pick from a few options. Before we go further, save a picture file to your desktop as "picture.jpg/png/whatever the file extension is". Let's introduce our user to the menu (using ECHO). Now, let's present our menu. Just do a series of ECHO statements, for example:

ECHO What would you like to do?
ECHO.
ECHO A. Say hello.
ECHO B. Open up a picture from the desktop.
ECHO C. End the program.
ECHO D. Start the program over.

Obviously, we are going to learn a few new tricks by doing this menu. Right now our program looks like... (Ignore the ":choice" for now)

```
menu - Notepad                                              _  □
File  Edit  Format  View  Help
@ECHO OFF
REM The above line removes excessive output.

REM This program was created on 7/21/2016.
REM This program was written by Matt DeSipio.
REM This program was written for Basic Programming Essentials.

REM Changing the window size to a larger size.
mode con: cols=160 lines=78

REM Changing the colors of the window.
Color OF

REM Setting X equal to 4.
SET X=4
REM Setting Y equal to 4.
SET Y=4

IF %X% EQU %Y% (
        ECHO X and Y are equal!
)

REM Creating a pause.
ECHO.
PAUSE
ECHO.

:choiceD

ECHO what would you like to do?
ECHO.
ECHO A. Say hello.
ECHO B. Open up a picture from the desktop.
ECHO C. End the program.
ECHO D. Start the program over.
ECHO.
```

But right now, the program isn't a functional menu at all. To make it functional, we need to create a variable and have the user pick an option by assigning a value to that variable. We will then take that variable through a series of IF statements.

So let's create the variable "CHOICE" and let the user's decisions be stored to that variable. Add the line *SET /P CHOICE=Please enter your choice here, then press ENTER:* . Now the user can make a choice, and whatever decision they make will be stored as "CHOICE".

Now that "CHOICE" carries the value of our user's option, we can put it through a series of IF statements.

IF CHOICE EQU A (do choice A stuff)
IF CHOICE EQU B (do choice B stuff)
IF CHOICE EQU C (do choice C stuff)
IF CHOICE EQU D (do choice D stuff)

So let's go into our file, and under where the user made their decision put the code: (Note: the "/I" ("I" as in "igloo") allows a lowercase or uppercase entry)

IF /I %CHOICE% EQU A (
ECHO Thank you for saying hello.
ECHO Hello to you as well.
)

If the user entered "A" (or "a"), the window will display the text we have entered. If the user did not enter "A", the program will not go into the IF statement (and skip over it) because CHOICE does not equal "A".

What about if the user enters "B"? Do you know how to open a file? Use the START command followed by the file pathway. Learning about file pathways is interesting, but really it's just the location of where the file is in the computer.

The line of code would be *START ""* *"C:\Users\mdesipio\Desktop\picture.jpg"*. Obviously your pathway will be a little different unless your username is mdesipio. You can change the pathway to open any file (and any type of file) anywhere on your computer. Enjoy.

IF /I %CHOICE% EQU B (
START "" "C:\Users\mdesipio\Desktop\picture.jpg"
)

To be able to do choices C and D, we need learn about "goto" and "EOF". "C" is easy to do, since the user wants to end the program, we have to "send" our program to "EOF", or "end of file". To do this, the code is simply...

IF /I %CHOICE% EQU C (
goto:EOF
)

Now if the user selects "C" the program will be ended. Surely if we can "send" our file to "EOF", we can "send" our file to other places in the program. If the user selects "D", the file will be started over. First, we have to go back into our code and add a location. This is done by adding ":location" to where you want the location. Let's go into our file and add a location "choiceD" to our text before the menu.

Now type the code for choice D...

IF /I %CHOICE% EQU D (
goto:choiceD
)

At the end of the file add some spaces, thank you messages, and whatever you want. This program is now functional.

```
IF %X% EQU %Y% (
        ECHO X and Y are equal!
)

REM Creating a pause.
ECHO.
PAUSE
ECHO.

:choiceD

ECHO What would you like to do?
ECHO.
ECHO A. Say hello.
ECHO B. Open up a picture from the desktop.
ECHO C. End the program.
ECHO D. Start the program over.
ECHO.

REM Setting CHOICE.
SET /P CHOICE=Please enter your choice here, then press ENTER:

REM Choice A
IF /I %CHOICE% EQU A (
        ECHO.
        ECHO Thank you for saying hello.
        ECHO Hello to you as well.
        ECHO.
)

REM Choice B
IF /I %CHOICE% EQU B (
        START "" "C:\Users\mdesipio\Desktop\picture.jpg"
        ECHO.
)

REM Choice C
IF /I %CHOICE% EQU C (
        goto:EOF
)

REM Choice D
IF /I %CHOICE% EQU D (
        ECHO.|
        goto:choiceD
)

REM Creating a pause.
PAUSE
```

```
C:\WINDOWS\system32\cmd.exe

X and Y are equal!

Press any key to continue . . .

What would you like to do?

A. Say hello.
B. Open up a picture from the desktop.
C. End the program.
D. Start the program over.

Please enter your choice here, then press ENTER: d

What would you like to do?

A. Say hello.
B. Open up a picture from the desktop.
C. End the program.
D. Start the program over.

Please enter your choice here, then press ENTER: A

Thank you for saying hello.
Hello to you as well.

Press any key to continue . . .
```

Congratulations, you are becoming much better at BATCH! Note how the "/I" allowed both lowercase and uppercase entries to work. BATCH is case sensitive, so usually if you declare a variable as "RESULT", using "result" will not work. Remember this if you ever have to troubleshoot a non-functioning program - it is a good place to start checking since it is a common mistake.

Chapter 5: FOR loops

IF statements are not trivial, but I did say "relatively easy" for a reason. FOR loops do tend to be a little more difficult and a little more difficult to see a purpose for unless you are writing complex programs.

A FOR loop tells the program, "Do something for as many times as I tell you too". For loops in BATCH can have a couple of different applications/syntaxes. For our purposes, we will use "/l" ("l" as in "Ladder") but there are many others you can use for different applications. In FOR loops, instead of using the normal %variable% setup (%x% in our case), we use the %%variable setup (or %%x). This applies to FOR loops only.

The basic syntax is *FOR /l %%x in (start, step, end) do (something here)*. The start is the first number the FOR loop begins at, the step is how much it goes up by each round, and end is where the for loop stops. For example, *FOR /l %%x in (1, 1, 10) do (something)* means "Do *something* for X values of 1, 2, 3, 4, 5, 6, 7, 8, 9, and 10". Open up a new Notepad file and type the following code after adding everything else you need/want.

FOR /l %%X in (1,1,10) do (echo %%X)

Run your file and you will see the window print 1-10. This is because the first time the FOR loop was run through, X=1. The program then went through the loop again, but since the step was 1, X=2 now. Then it went to X=3, and so on. Please remember that BATCH is case sensitive so keep all variables uppercase or lowercase - having a program not run because you mixed "X" and "x" can cause a lot of frustration!

For loops can be very useful and save a lot of time. For example, instead of our code being...

ECHO 1
ECHO 2
ECHO 3
ECHO 4
ECHO 5
ECHO 6
ECHO 7
ECHO 8
ECHO 9
ECHO 10

It was just...

FOR /l %%X in (1,1,10) do (echo %%X).

Imagine if we wanted to print 1-100, just think about how much time this FOR loop would save us! A trick I like with FOR loops is testing to see if files exist. In the process, we will learn how to use EXIST.

Create a new folder on your desktop. Name it "TOP_SECRET". In that folder, create a series of text files named "#.txt". Make # equal to anything from 1 - 50. Do not create all 50, just create a few. I named mine 3.txt, 17.txt, and 41.txt, for example.

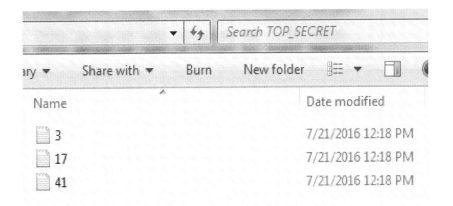

Let's have our program tell us what files exist.

```
FOR /l %%x in (1, 1, 50) do (
IF EXIST == C:\Users\mdesipio\Desktop\TOP_SECRET\%%x.txt (
ECHO %%x.txt
)
)
```

The above code will go into the TOP_SECRET folder and check to see what values of X a files exists for and print it out. Maybe this does not seem all that useful on the surface, but imagine if you worked for a company with thousands of part numbers. Using this program, you could see all the files you have in a folder that start with a part number. As you can imagine (and will see later in the big example), this program could be edited easily in such a way that the user could type a part number and have the program show all the files that exist for that part number.

The first time the program runs into the FOR loop, x=1. So x=1 runs into the IF statement and if "1.txt" exists, the program will print out "1.txt".

However, since "1.txt" does not exist (unless you made one of your files 1.txt), it never goes into the IF statement. Instead it skips right over it, and goes back to the beginning of the FOR loop and changes x to x=2.

Now do this, until x=3. When x=3, the program will go into the TOP_SECRET folder and see that "3.txt" does exist. So it will go into the IF statement and print out "3.txt" to the screen. The program then returns to the beginning and so on.

Our program looks like this right now... (Again... in your code, always use either a lowercase "x" or uppercase "X" - do not mix)

```
for - Notepad
File  Edit  Format  View  Help
@ECHO OFF
REM The above line removes excessive output.

REM This program was created on 7/21/2016.
REM This program was written by Matt DeSipio.
REM This program was written for Basic Programming Essentials.

REM Changing the window size to a larger size.
mode con: cols=160 lines=78

REM Changing the colors of the window.
Color OF

REM Creating start location.
:Start

REM Adding a heading.
ECHO The following programs exist...
ECHO.

REM Testing to see what files exist.
For /l %%x in (1, 1, 50) do (
        IF EXIST == C:\Users\mdesipio\Desktop\TOP_SECRET\%%x.txt
        ECHO %%x.txt
        )
)

REM Creating a pause.
ECHO.
PAUSE
```

FOR loops are a little more complicated, but the payoff is great once you find a true purpose for them.

Before we move on, let's allow the user to run the entire program over again if they choose to. We will use an IF statement and "goto" to accomplish this.

SET /P C=Would you like to run the program over again? (y/n):
IF /I %C% == Y (
goto:start
)

Be sure to add the location ":start" at the beginning of your file. Our program is now complete and looks like this (figure). We will use for loops again in our final BATCH example, so if you are confused, maybe one more example will help.

```
@ECHO OFF
REM The above line removes excessive output.

REM This program was created on 7/21/2016.
REM This program was written by Matt Desipio.
REM This program was written for Basic Programming Essentials.

REM Changing the window size to a larger size.
mode con: cols=160 lines=78

REM Changing the colors of the window.
Color 0F

REM Creating start location.
:Start

REM Adding a heading.
ECHO The following programs exist...
ECHO.

REM Testing to see what files exist.
For /l %%x in (1, 1, 50) do (
        IF EXIST == C:\Users\mdesipio\Desktop\TOP_SECRET\%%x.txt
        ECHO %%x.txt
        )
)

REM Creating a pause.
ECHO.
PAUSE
ECHO.

REM Allowing the user to run the program again if they wish.
Set /P C=Would you like to run the program over again? (y/n):

IF /I %C% == Y (
        ECHO.
        goto:start
)
```

```
C:\WINDOWS\system32\cmd.exe

The following programs exist...

3.txt
17.txt
41.txt

Press any key to continue . . .

Would you like to run the program over again? (y/n): y

The following programs exist...

3.txt
17.txt
41.txt

Press any key to continue . . .
```

Chapter 6: Writing to external files

Let's take a break from all this logic and get back to some simple steps. Let's have a program write text to a text file. It may seem like it going to be complicated, but it's fairly intuitive. The syntax is:

(Insert text here) >(>) file.txt.

You use a single ">" to create a new text file, or overwrite text. For example say you had...

(ECHO hi) > name.txt
(ECHO bye) > name.txt

If you opened the file name.txt, the file would only have "bye" in it. This is because the "bye" overwrote the "hi" since it came after it in the code. If you want to append text use two ">>".

(ECHO hi) >> name.txt
(ECHO bye) >> name.txt

Now if you opened name.txt (it will be on your desktop), it would read...

hi
bye

Open Notepad, and write the program set up as usual. Ask the user to input values for 3 variables. The program should look like...

File Edit Format View Help

```
@ECHO OFF
REM The above line removes excessive output.

REM This program was created on 7/21/2016.
REM This program was written by Matt DeSipio.
REM This program was written for Basic Programming Essentials.

REM Changing the window size to a larger size.
mode con: cols=160 lines=78

REM Changing the colors of the window.
Color 0F

REM Asking the user for A, B, and C.

SET /P A=Please enter the value for A:
SET /P B=Please enter the value for B:
SET /P C=Please enter the value for C:
```

Now let's print what the user entered to a text file. A tab separates the variables.

(ECHO %A%   %B%   %C%) >> test.txt

Do not forget a space after ECHO

If we open test.txt (it will be created automatically in the desktop if your batch file is saved to the desktop), we will see all three values the user entered. In this example, the user entered 2, 3, and 4.

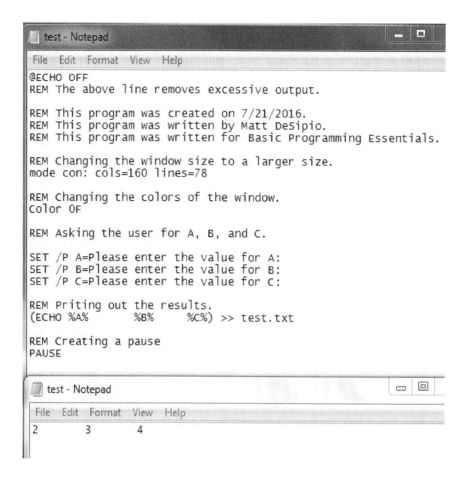

While we're at this, let's create a guestbook. Open Notepad. Proceed with the usual setup. Ask the user for their first name (fname), Middle initial (MI), last name (lname), and the rating of their experience with your business.

The program should look like this.

```
guest - Notepad
File  Edit  Format  View  Help

@ECHO OFF
REM The above line removes excessive output.

REM This program was created on 7/21/2016.
REM This program was written by Matt DeSipio.
REM This program was written for Basic Programming Essentials.

REM Changing the window size to a larger size.
mode con: cols=160 lines=78

REM Changing the colors of the window.
Color 0F

REM Setting start location.
:start

REM Asking for the guest's name.
ECHO.
ECHO Valued Guest,
ECHO.
SET /P fname=Please type your first name, then press ENTER:
SET /P MI=Please type your middle intial, then press ENTER:
SET /P lname=Please type your last name, then press ENTER:
ECHO.

REM Asking the gues to rate their experience.
SET /P RATE=On a scale of 1-5 how would you rate your experience? (1-5):
ECHO.
ECHO Thank you. Your answers will be recorded.

REM Printing it out to an external file.
(ECHO %fname%   %MI%    %lname% %RATE%) >> guest.txt

ECHO.

goto:start
```

Notice how the program always goes back to the original question after (the goto:start loop). This would make sure that all guests would have to do is type their name and their rating and hit enter. Notice how the text file the results get printed to has some headings this time. I created the guest.txt text file before running the program, and typed the headings, with a tab in-between.

```
C:\WINDOWS\system32\cmd.exe

Valued Guest,

Please type your first name, then press ENTER: Matt
Please type your middle intial, then press ENTER: M
Please type your last name, then press ENTER: DeSipio

On a scale of 1-5 how would you rate your experience? (1-5): 2

Thank you. Your answers will be recorded.

Valued Guest,

Please type your first name, then press ENTER: John
Please type your middle intial, then press ENTER: K
Please type your last name, then press ENTER: Doe

On a scale of 1-5 how would you rate your experience? (1-5): 5

Thank you. Your answers will be recorded.

Valued Guest,

Please type your first name, then press ENTER: Missy
Please type your middle intial, then press ENTER: D
Please type your last name, then press ENTER: Hunter

On a scale of 1-5 how would you rate your experience? (1-5): 3

Thank you. Your answers will be recorded.

Valued Guest,

Please type your first name, then press ENTER:
```

The great thing about writing to an external text file is that you can import the data into excel and make graphs and other representations of the data. Maybe this data could be valuable to a business.

```
guest - Notepad

File   Edit   Format   View   Help

Fname     M.I.      Lname     RATING

Matt      M         DeSipio   2
John      K         Doe       5
Missy     D         Hunter    3
```

Chapter 7: Big Example

The example program will begin at the first "@ECHO OFF".

This program requires that some text files be added to the TOP_SECRET folder. This program will allow the user to enter a part number and a quantity, and the program will open a file that displays information about part number and quantity combo.

Go into the folder and save text files as "partnumber-quantitypcs.txt". For example, I saved:

"3-2pcs.txt"
"7-1pcs.txt"
"9-3pcs.txt"
"1-49pcs.txt"
"4-5pcs.txt"
"10-10pcs.txt"
"2-21pcs.txt"
"5-9pcs.txt"
"4-29pcs.txt"
"6-50pcs.txt"
"8-13pcs.txt"

Make sure you have a file for each part number 1-10, if you want to do multiple files for a part number feel free to do so, notice how 4 has two files. We can imagine this program might be useful to some businesses. Say your company sells parts with part numbers 32981-99832. If an employee needed to pull up information about a specific part number and quantity combination (say previous orders), this program would automatically open the file based on the user entries.

Now that all that is done, the program should run smoothly, enjoy and have fun creating your own files. See if you can teach yourself how to use the ELSE command. Note that it must be placed right after the closing parenthesis for the previous IF statement (no ENTER allowed). Only use ELSE when you are using one IF statement. For example – ELSE would not work well in our menu program since there are 4 IF's. Also pay attention to the indenting and overall organization/presentation.

Note that BATCH programming can get far more complex than what we have covered here. We have, however, set a solid foundation for you to continue learning BATCH if you ever want to.

PROGRAM STARTS NEXT LINE

```
@ECHO OFF
REM Turning off excessive output.

REM This program was created on 6/16/2016 by Matt DeSipio.
REM This program enables users to easily pull up the file they need.
REM The file that will be brought up will display information about the part + quantity.
REM This program works for part numbers 1-10.

REM Editing window size to make the window larger.
mode con: cols=160 lines=78

REM Changing the colors of the program to make it easier to read.
Color 0F

REM Creating extra space.
ECHO.

REM Welcoming the user.
ECHO * * * * * WELCOME TO THE 1-10 FILE LAUNCHER * * * * * *

REM ---------------- Setting location start ---------------------
:start

REM Creating extra space
ECHO.

REM Storing the user inputted response as variable A - this is the part number.
SET /P A=Please type your part number, then press ENTER:

REM Creating extra space.
ECHO.

        REM Creating IF statements to make sure part number is valid for this program.

                IF %A% LEQ 0 (
                        ECHO Your part number is not valid for this program.
                        ECHO This program only works for part numbers 1-10.
                        ECHO Hit any key to exit.
                        ECHO.
                        PAUSE
                        goto:EOF
                )

                IF %A% GEQ 11 (
                        ECHO Your part number is not valid for this program.
                        ECHO This program only works for part numbers 1-10.
                        ECHO Hit any key to exit.
                        ECHO.
                        PAUSE
                        goto:EOF
```

```
                )
REM Making the layout look organized.
ECHO ----------------------------------------------------------------------------
ECHO.

REM ---------------------- Setting quan location ----------------------------
:quan

        REM Storing the user inputted response as variable B - this is the quantity
        SET /P B=Please type Quantity, then press ENTER:

        REM Checking to see if a file exists for what the user has entered.
        IF EXIST == C:\Users\mdesipio\Desktop\TOP_SECRET\%A%-%B%pcs.txt (
                ECHO.
                ECHO FILE EXISTS...
        ) ELSE (
                ECHO.

                REM Displaying what files exist for the entered p/n.
                ECHO ERROR 001 -
                ECHO FILES FOR P/N %A% CURRENTLY ONLY EXIST IN QUANTITIES OF...
                ECHO.
                For /l %%x in (0, 1, 50) do (
                        IF EXIST == C:\Users\mdesipio\Desktop\TOP_SECRET\%A%-%%xpcs.txt (
                        ECHO %%x
                        )
                )
                ECHO.

                goto:quan
        )

        REM Creating extra space
        ECHO.
        ECHO.

ECHO ============== Pressing any key will launch your file ==================

        REM Creating extra space.
        ECHO.
        ECHO.

        REM Creating a pause so the user can review entries.
        PAUSE

        REM Opening the file.
        Start "" "C:\Users\mdesipio\Desktop\TOP_SECRET\%A%-%B%pcs.txt"

        REM Creating extra space.
        ECHO.


        ECHO.

        REM Writing to an external text file to keep records.
        (ECHO %B%        %A%) >> record_of_1to10.txt

        REM Allowing the user to run the program over again - if desired.
        SET /P C=Would you like to run this program over again? (y/n):

        IF /I %C% == Y (
                ECHO.
                ECHO.
                ECHO ========================================================
                ECHO ********************************************************
                ECHO ========================================================
                goto start
        )
```

```
C:\WINDOWS\system32\cmd.exe

* * * * * * * * * * * * * * * WELCOME TO THE 1-10 FILE LAUNCHER * * *
Please type your part number, then press ENTER: 9
-------------------------------------------------------------------

Please type Quantity, then press ENTER: 12
ERROR 001 -
FILES FOR P/N 9 CURRENTLY ONLY EXIST IN QUANTITIES OF...
3
Please type Quantity, then press ENTER: 3
FILE EXISTS...

=============================== Pressing any key will launch your file =

Press any key to continue . . .
```

PART 2 - HTML Programming

Chapter 8: How to create, save, and open HTML files

The process for creating HTML files is very similar to how we created BATCH files. There is only one difference. Instead of saving the file as a ".bat" file, you save it as an ".html" file. We will still use Notepad, although you may want to search for another text editor - there are many available to download online.

In HTML code, we use tags. Tags look like "<tag>". Open up notepad. Let's type <p>Hello, World!</p> in the first line. Save the file as HelloWorld.html to your desktop.

Right click the icon on your desktop and "open with" some internet option. Congratulations, you just created your first HTML file.

Or final website will look like...

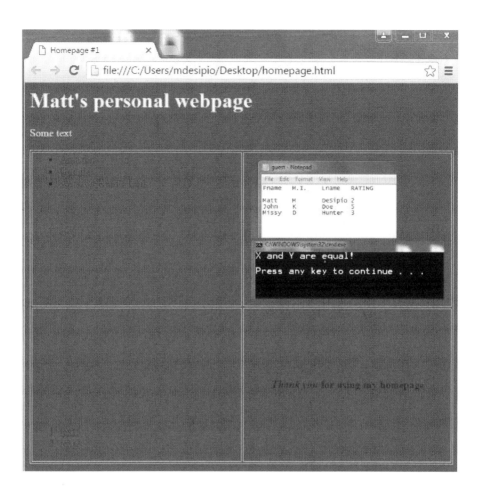

Chapter 9: Example homepage for your PC/LAPTOP

This quick instructional will show you how to make a very basic website using only notepad and basic HTML code. These websites will not be public and will be on your computer for you to view only. These private websites serve as useful homepages and making them serves as a fun hobby. In the process of doing this you will also learn HTML code and some more basic programming skills and techniques. You can even set the webpage you make to be the website that appears when you open the internet. Websites can obviously get far more complex than what we will cover - if you are interested in that you should learn about JavaScript. We will not cover that here.

When writing in HTML code, we use tags. Tags look like something inside "< >". The first tag we will learn is the most important tag, <HTML>. This tag will let us start making a real webpage. For every tag we have, we will need a tag that closes that tag. So the tag that closes <HTML> is </HTML>. Tags that close out tags have the general form of something inside "</ >". Let's make our second website by using just these tags.

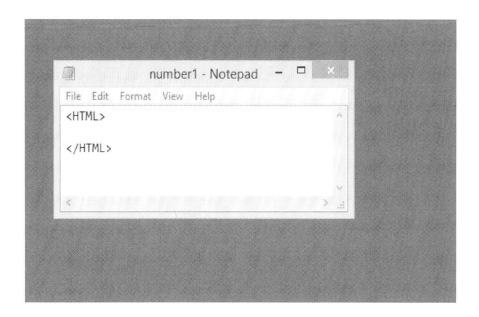

When you open this page as a website, it is a blank page - but it is still a website. You will notice that your URL is something like...

"C:\Users**YourName**\Desktop\number1.html".

This is because the webpage is only yours and is not online at all, it will come up even without an internet connection. It is only a file on your computer. Right now our website looks like:

<HTML>
</HTML>.

Why don't we add some body tags? Whenever we add tags, we always want to place the opening and closing tags in between other tags. So if we add body tags, it will look like:

<HTML>
<Body>
</Body>
</HTML>

Now, our website still looks the same, but if we make a minor adjustment to the opening body tag, we can add a background color. To add a background color, we have to include a command into the opening body tag – ***bgcolor=color***. Here, whatever "color" you choose will be the background color. We can do some basic colors with this. Let's try blue, but you're welcome to try any color and see if it works.

```
<HTML>
<body bgcolor=blue>
</body>
</HTML>
```

Now if we open our file again, using **right click > Open with > Internet explorer**, we see a webpage!

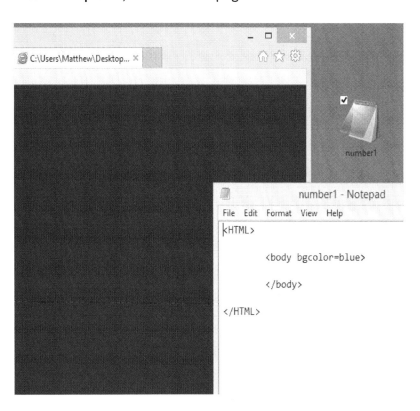

Note that it is good practice to use the indenting and spacing you see. It may not be clear now, but when our webpages start to get complicated, we will want this organization. Comments are also a big part of this organization (any similarities to Batch?). Comments help us remember why we did certain things when we look back at this code in a year. It might not seem immediately obvious why we do this now, but it will be handy in the future. To add a comment in HTML code we do the below.

<!-- This is a comment in HTML code -->

Let's see what our webpage code looks like with comments added.

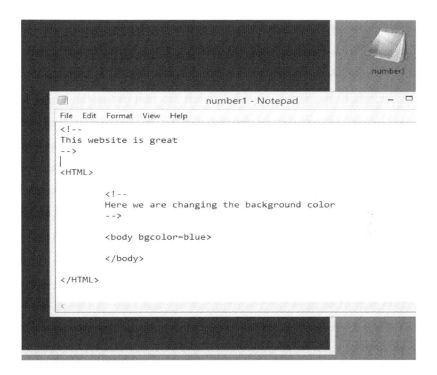

So now we can really start learning how to build a homepage for you. Let's first add a heading and some text under that heading. Let's make sure the text under the heading has parts that are bold, italicized, and underlined so we can learn some more tags. If we want to make a heading, we use the tag <h1>. Everything we do now will be in between the body tags. So if we want to add the heading "My Homepage", we will put <h1>My Heading</h1> in our code. Please note that you can add a title tag before the body tag to change the words on the tab. You will see this in the final website.

To add normal text to our page, we use the tags <p> to open up and </p> to close it out (as we saw with our hello, world program). If we want to add "this webpage is awesome", we will add ***<p>this webpage is awesome</p>*** to the code. BUT, we want to do better than this. Why don't we underline "is" (tags <u> and </u>), bold "awesome" (tags <b> and </b>), and italicize "this" (tags <i> and </i>). So putting this all together, if we want to add this text under our heading, the corresponding code will be:

"<p><i>This</i> webpage <u>is</u> <b>awesome</b></p>".

Be sure not to forget spaces! When using most tags, it is useful to think that everything between the opening and closing tags is affected by the tag. So let's put this all together and see our website.

Personally, I don't like this color scheme. So let's change it up. Let's go with a dark blue background and a golden yellow text. We cannot just type in the color next to the "bgcolor=". It will not work all the time. In order to use these colors we have to use color codes. You can find them online very easily by searching HTML color codes. The code for the dark blue I want is "0101DF" and the code for the golden yellow I want is "#FFFF00". You can pick any colors you want.

Now we have to go and change/add some code. The first step is easy. To change the background color from blue to 0101DF (dark blue) we change the existing <body bgcolor=blue> to the new <body bgcolor=0101DF>.

To change the font color of the text, we have to add some font tags (<font> and </font>). But we also have to include some commands within our tags again. Since we are changing both the heading's font color and the text's font color, we can put the opening font tag before the heading and the closing tag after the text. Note if you wanted them to be different colors, you could just open a font tag with the color command before the heading and close it after the heading and do the same with a different color for the text. We will keep both the same color.

So how do we change the text color? Say, for example, we want to change the color of "*text*". In HTML this is done by:

<font color="color choice">
Text
</font>.

This will change the color of *text* to whatever color you want. Let's go ahead and change some colors in our webpage. You can use quotation marks but you do not have to. I just included both ways to show that both work.

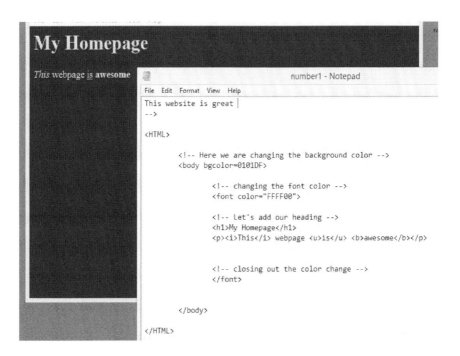

Now that we have the basic structure of our webpage down, let's add a table. Let's just have this table be a 2x2 table. Let's have a list of links to websites in one part, pictures In another, some links to open text files in one, and some thank you text to the user in the last section.

So how do we add tables in HTML? We need a couple of tags, the first tags we need will be a table tag (<table> and </table>). Everything that goes in between these tags will be in our table. To start and end a row we need the <tr> and </tr> tags, respectively. To start and end new columns within a row, use the <td> and </td> tags, respectively. For simplicity's sake, we will make every row have the same amount of columns (a 2x2 table).

So before we go ahead and add this code to our file, let's see the basic structure of a table in HTML.

```
<table>
<tr>
<td> row 1 column 1 </td>
<td> row 1 column 2 </td>
</tr>
<tr>
<td> row 2 column 1 </td>
<td> row 2 column 2 </td>
</tr>
</table>
```

Please note that you should use the proper indentation you see in the pictures. I just did it like this so it would stay readable in electronic format. This is the general form of a 2x2 table in HTML, let's add this to our webpage code and see what it looks like. Often, it is easiest to have both notepad and the webpage open at the same time. You can just save the notepad with the new code and refresh the webpage to observe the changes.

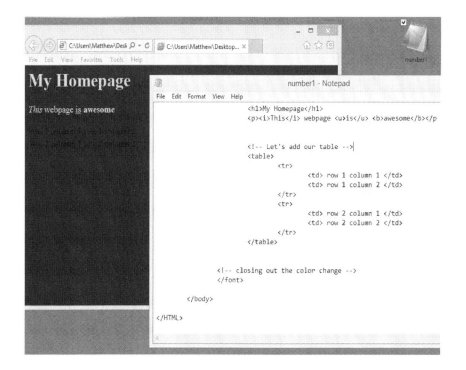

Note that now that our webpage code is getting longer, we will no longer show the entire code, just the new pieces of it. Notice how the text in the table was not affected by the font tags even though the table is within the font tags. We will figure out how to solve this in a little. We can see that our table is pretty basic but that it works. Let's add a border to it, so we can see the structure of the table better. To add a border we just need to add the "border=#" command within the table tag, with "#" being whatever size you want the thickness of the table to be. For example, let's add "border = 1" to our table tag and see the difference.

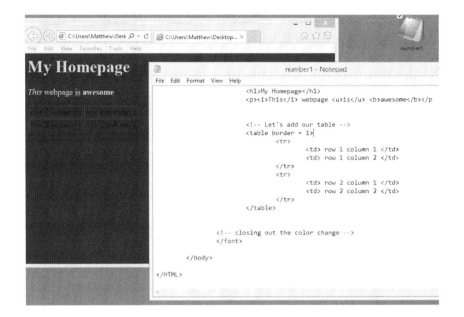

Now that we've got the basic structure of our table, let's figure out how to change the color of the table text and add some things in that table. First we will change the colors, then we will add some links to one piece of the table.

To change the color of the text, just simply add the <font color="FFFF00"> tag before the text, but after the <td> and add the </font> tag after the text and before the </td> tag. This looks like this.

This is nice, but let's do something more interesting. Let's first change our text color to the dark blue we used in the background. Then let's make the background color of the table the golden yellow we used in the text. Let's see this result both with and without the table border. To change the background color of the table, simply add "bgcolor=color" to the table tag.

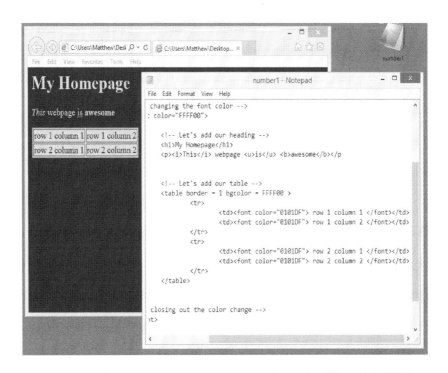

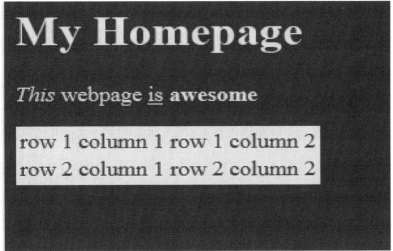

Let's continue with our homepage without using table borders (you can change the color of the border using the "bordercolor=color" command within the table tag). Now we want to start adding things to this table, but first, let's space it out and make it look more presentable. Let's change the code in our file to:

```
<table Width="100%" bgcolor = FFFF00 >
<tr>
<td align = "center" width="50%"><font color="0101DF"> row 1
column 1 </font></td>
<td align = "center" width="50%"><font color="0101DF"> row 1
column 2 </font></td>
</tr>
<tr>
<td align = "center" width="50%"><font color="0101DF"> row 2
column 1 </font></td>
<td align = "center" width="50%"><font color="0101DF"> row 2
column 2 </font></td>
</tr>
</table>
```

To make the table take up the entire width of the screen, we use the "width = "100%"" inside the <table> to do so. After doing this, we add "width="50%"" to all the <td> tags to make each section of our table take up half the width of the screen. The "align = "center"", is used to align our text to make it look better (you can also experiment with "valign" if you wish). If we do all these changes, our webpage now looks like the image below.

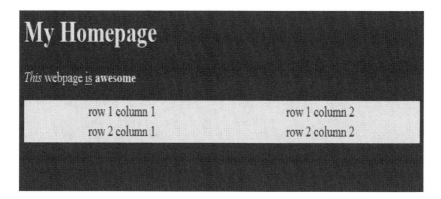

To add links to our page, let's replace "row 1 column 1" with:

```
<ul type="square">
<li><a href="URL OF SITE" target = "_blank">what link will be in
webpage</a></li>
<li><a href="URL OF SITE" target = "_blank">what link will be in
webpage</a></li>
</ul>
```

The <ul> and </ul> tags create an unnumbered list. The <ol> and
</ol> tags will create an ordered, numbered list. In the next section
of our table, we can insert some images. We need to follow the
following syntax...

<img src="file pathway" alt="text" height="#/%" width="#/%">

We will create another table inside of this section, but this time this
table will have no border. The table will have 2 rows and 1 column.
My pathway will be "C:\Users\mdesipio\Desktop\Filter Mount
Project" and I named my picture files 1.png and 2.png. Note it may
be best to use a pathway that does not have spaces involved (this is
why you see some people add underscores in folder names to
replace spaces - generally spaces are not your friend). Our
homepage code now looks like (Please note that the
indenting/spacing/colors/table format have changed somewhat,
this is to show that the presentation of the code does not affect the
website - you can use whatever spacing/indentation you find
best)...

```
<table width=100% height=75% border=1 bordercolor=white>
    <tr>
        <td>
            <ul>
                <li><a href="url">link text</a></li>
                <li><a href="url">link text</a></li>
                <li><a href="url">link text</a></li>
            </ul>
        </td>

        <td>
            <TABLE border=0>
                <tr>
                    <td><img src="C:\Users\mdesipio\Desktop\Filter Mount Project\1.png" alt="1"></td>
                </tr>
                <tr>
                    <td><img src="C:\Users\mdesipio\Desktop\Filter Mount Project\2.png" alt="2"></td>
                </tr>
            </TABLE>
        </td>
    </tr>
    <tr>
        <td>

        </td>

        <td>

        </td>
    </tr>
</table>
```

We have two more sections of our table left to fill up. Since we are not using JavaScript, HTML is pretty limited. That being said, there are definitely a couple of things left to learn in HTML. Let's have the next section of our table open up a text file. We need to add this...

<a href="pathway" target="_self">text</a>

Let's make another list, and have a couple of files available. This time let's use an ordered list, <ol>.

```
<table width=100% height=75% border=1 bordercolor=white>
    <tr>
        <td>
            <ul>
                <li><a href="url">link text</a></li>
                <li><a href="url">link text</a></li>
                <li><a href="url">link text</a></li>
            </ul>
        </td>

        <td>
            <TABLE border=0>
                <tr>
                    <td><img src="C:\Users\mdesipio\Desktop\Filter Mount Project\1.png" alt="1"></td>
                </tr>
                <tr>
                    <td><img src="C:\Users\mdesipio\Desktop\Filter Mount Project\2.png" alt="2"></td>
                </tr>
            </TABLE>
        </td>
    </tr>
    <tr>
        <td>
            <ol>
                <li><a href="pathway" target="_self">text</a></li>
                <li><a href="pathway" target="_self">text</a></li>
            </ol>
        </td>

        <td>

        </td>
    </tr>
</table>
```

In our final section, let's simply thank the user for using your homepage. Now let's clean up the appearance of our table again. Go into the <td> tags and add a *width=50%* and a *height=50%* if that is the look you desire. You can also add align (horizontal alignment) and valign (vertical alignment) features again. You can also change the width and height of the images. All of this was done to show these features. Enjoy making yourself a simple homepage that might help make some things easier for you - such as being able to click the links to your favorite sites.

```
homepage - Notepad
File  Edit  Format  View  Help
<HTML>
<TITLE>Homepage #1</TITLE>
<BODY BGCOLOR=red>
<!--
Personal homepage created on 7/25/2016 for Matt DeSipio.
-->
<font color=white><H1>Matt's personal webpage</H2></font>
<font color=white><p>Some text</p></font>
<table width=100% height=75% border=1 bordercolor=white>
        <tr>
                <td valign=top width=50% height=50%>
                        <ul>
                                <li><a href="https://www.amazon.com/">Amazon</a></li>
                                <li><a href="https://www.google.com/">Google</a></li>
                                <li><a href="https://www.amazon.com/Kindle-eBooks/b?ie=UTF8&node=154606011">Amazon Kindle Link</a></li>
                        </ul>
                </td>
                <td valign=center align=center width=50% height=50%>
                        <TABLE border=0>
                                <tr>
                                        <td><img src="C:\Users\mdesipio\Desktop\Filter Mount Project\1.png" alt="1" height=70%></td>
                                </tr>
                                <tr>
                                        <td><img src="C:\Users\mdesipio\Desktop\Filter Mount Project\2.png" alt="2" height=70%></td>
                                </tr>
                        </TABLE>
                </td>
        </tr>
        <tr>
                <td valign=bottom width=50% height=50%>
                        <ol>
                                <li><a href=C:\users\mdesipio\Desktop\test1.txt target="_self">text1</a></li>
                                <li><a href=C:\users\mdesipio\Desktop\test2.txt target="_self">text2</a></li>
                        </ol>
                </td>
                <td valign=center align=center width=50% height=50%>
                        <p><b><i>Thank you</i> for using my homepage</b></p>
                </td>
        </tr>
</table>
</BODY>
</HTML>
```

You have successfully learned the basics to HTML programming. In your file, you should have more comment lines. The webpage looks as follows...

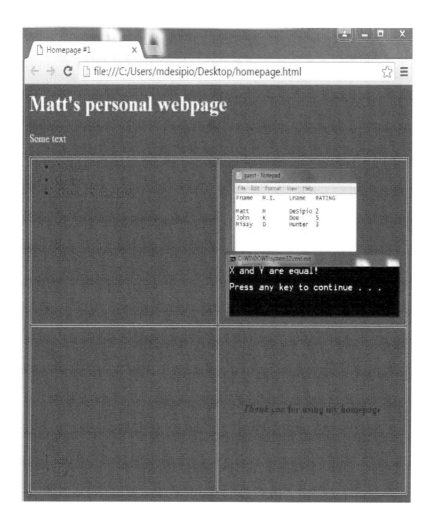

Matt's personal webpage

Some text

PART 3 – C programming

Chapter 10: Set up + Hello, World!

C programming is a non-trivial programming language that has many practical applications. C programming requires a compiler. On Ubuntu, (Ubuntu is a free Operating System) you can compile C programs for free. On windows, I am not sure you can. I will use the free compiling method on the Ubuntu Operating System to show what the output of the program would look like. I will also be using a different text editor so you can see the benefits of having one. This discussion on C will be briefer than the discussion on BATCH, because you should pull knowledge from the BATCH section and apply it here.

Just like in BATCH and HTML, comment lines in C programming are very important. A comment line in C starts with "//". For example...

// This is a comment line in C programming.

To get a C programming running, you need certain "includes". To start, we definitely need "stdio.h".

#include <stdio.h>

Now, we need to create the body of our program.

void main (void){
// Program main
}

ECHO in BATCH, does the same as *printf("text")* in C. To continue tradition, let's have the first line of your program read "Hello, World!" Your code should look something like...

#include <stdio.h>
void main(void){
//Program main

Printf("Hello, World");
}

Semicolons should go at the end of every line in C programming. If you had a way to run the file, you would see "Hello, World!" display on the screen. On the Ubuntu operating system you can compile the program by opening the terminal typing "gcc filename.c -o filename" and then typing "./filename". The program must be saved as "filename.c" for it to run as a C program.

Chapter 11: Big Example

11.1 Includes + Defines

Now that we have the basic setup ready, we can really start to learn some of the syntax to get a C program doing something. We will create another menu program. This program will be very similar to the program we wrote in BATCH programming earlier. We will do this so we can see how what we learned earlier, can be useful even in different programming languages.

Any good C program, will require a little better setup than what the hello world file required. Firstly, we need more and better comment lines. Go ahead and open a new file and type some specific comment lines before we get started.

Now we will want to include some more items. Let's include stdio.h, stdlib.h, ctype.h, and math.h. Note that we may or may not use these in our program, but these are good ones to include.

Now we will want to add some defines. Since this is an introductory text, we will not go into great detail about defines or includes. We want to define PI (even though we may not use it - it is still a good example) and N (we will use it for variables that we want to contain a string of text). To define something we have to use #define followed by that variable we want to define (Pi or n), followed by what defines it. So to define PI, we will use the fact that the arccosine of -1.0 is PI. Note that if you use PI in your program you would have to do this so PI can be used. PI is not automatically recognized. We will define N to be 64 and this is good practice.

#define n 64
#define PI acos(-1.0)

Now that we have our includes and our defines, we can start our program. The code we have right now looks like the below image.

Take note of the color coding and automatic indenting the text editor provides.

```c
// This program was created by Matt DeSipio
// This program was created on 7/24/2016
// This program was created for Basic Programming Essentials
// This program will ask the user for a choice and do something with that choice

// INCLUDES SECTION
#include <stdio.h>
#include <stdlib.h>
#include <ctype.h>
#include <math.h>

// DEFINES SECTION
#define N 64
#define PI acos(-1.0)

// Program main
void main(void) {
    |
}
```

11.2 Variables

First, let's welcome the user and ask for their first name. We can welcome the user using the *printf* command. Asking the user for their name requires storing user inputted information as a variable. We saw how to do this in BATCH...

SET /P firstname=What is your first name? :

But how is this done in C? In C, we must first establish the variables we are going to use in the program. We know we are going to need a variable for their first name (fname). Since we are running a menu program, we know the user is going to have to enter a choice (CHOICE). Let's also ask the user for their GPA (GPA) and age (AGE). We now have 4 different variables that we are going to use. For our basic purposes, let's say there are 4 different types of variables in C (integers, doubles, characters, and strings).

Since fname is the user's first name, it is going to be stored as string of characters (If you wanted to ask for a single letter – you would store it is a character). Since GPA will be stored as a number with decimal points, it will be stored as a double. Since CHOICE and AGE are integers, they will be stored as integers.

In C, you should declare the variables you are going to be using before the program code starts. To store something as a string or character, type the variable after the text "char". To store something as an integer, type the variable after the text "int". To store something as a double, type the variable name after the text "double".

To store fname as a string we would type...

Char fname[N];

Notice how the string is followed by the letter "N" that we defined in the "defines" section enclosed by brackets. This is only for strings, single characters do not require this.

To store AGE as an integer we would type...

Int AGE;

To store GPA as a double we would type...

Double GPA;

Do not forget semicolons! Now that we have declared all of the variables we are going to use, we can proceed with our program. Right now, the code looks like...

```
// This program was created by Matt DeSipio
// This program was created on 7/24/2016
// This program was created for Basic Programming Essentials
// This program will ask the user for a choice and do something with that choice

// INCLUDES SECTION
#include <stdio.h>
#include <stdlib.h>
#include <ctype.h>
#include <math.h>

// DEFINES SECTION
#define N 64
#define PI acos(-1.0)

// Program main
void main(void) {
  // Variable declarations
  char fname[N];
  int AGE, CHOICE;
  double GPA;
```

Now that the first name variable is declared, we can ask the user to input data to it. First we have to ask the question to the user using *printf*. As we did in batch, put a space after the colon to make the entry look clean. In C programming using "\n" within a printf command will create an extra space in the output in a similar way to how "ECHO." created a space in BATCH. ("\t" creates a tab when inserted in a printf command just like "\n")

//Storing a user answered question as a string
printf("Please enter your first name here: ");

Now we must clear the computer of previously entered text (simply put) and scan in the user's entry and store it as a variable. To flush standard input...

fflush(stdin);

It is a good idea to add this code before you scan in a character or string. To scan in the user's answer and store it as a variable, we must use *scanf*. Since we are storing the data as a string, we will use *scanf("%s",&variable)*. Since firstname is a string, we have to store the entry at fname[0].

scanf("%s",&fname[0]);

It is clear, this process is a bit more involved than the process in BATCH. To store a single character (say last name initial), we would use...

//Storing a user answered question as a character
printf("\nPlease enter your last name initial here: ");
fflush(stdin);
scanf("%c",&lname);

Again, do not forget semicolons! Forgetting semicolons is a very popular mistake and is the cause for many errors in programs. Note how "%c" was used this time as lname is a single character and not a string.

To display the value of a variable to the screen, we use the printf command and use the type of variable (%s, %c, %d, %lf) in the statement instead of the actual variable and recall the variable outside of the quotes. Follow the basic format (for strings we use &variable[0] instead of just variable).

printf("the thing you entered is: %d,%lf,%c, or %s",variable);

Our program now welcomes the users and asks for and displays their first name.

```
// DEFINES SECTION
#define N 64
#define PI acos(-1.0)

// Program main
void main(void) {
    // Variable declarations
    char fname[N];
    int AGE, CHOICE;
    double GPA;

    printf("\nWelcome to this C program!\n\n");

    //Storing a user answered question as a word
    printf("Please enter your first name here: ");
    fflush(stdin);
    scanf("%s",&fname[0]);

    printf("\n\nHello, %s",&fname[0]);
```

Notice how the code includes "\n" inside the *printf* commands. You can have multiple "\n\n" in a *printf* to create additional space as well. I will change the amount of "\n"'s as the program progresses to change the way the program reads to the user.

Now let's present a menu of choices to our user. Let's use *printf* and some "\n"'s to create space.

Printf("\n\nPlease select your option...\n\n");
Printf("1. Evaluate your GPA\n");
Printf("2. Skip to the end\n");
Printf("3. Evaluate your age\n");

Now we have to ask the user for their choice and store their choice as variable "choice".

printf("What is your choice?: ");
scanf("%d",&choice);

Note that with integers and doubles, you do not have to flush standard input. Notice how "%d" was used to store the variable as an integer. Our program now asks the user for their name, and allows them to make a choice and stores that choice as a variable "choice".

```c
// Program main
void main(void) {
  // Variable declarations
  char fname[N];
  int AGE, CHOICE;
  double GPA;

  printf("\nWelcome to this C program!\n\n");

  //Storing a user answered question as a word
  printf("Please enter your first name here: ");
  fflush(stdin);
  scanf("%s",&fname[0]);

  printf("\nHello, %s",&fname[0]);

  printf("\n\nPlease select your option...\n\n");
  printf("1. Evaluate your GPA\n");
  printf("2. Skip to the end\n");
  printf("3. Evaluate your age\n");

  printf("What is your choice?: ");
  scanf("%d",&CHOICE);

}
```

```
mmdesipio@mmdesipio Inspiron 3130:~/Documents/Programming/C$ gcc BPE.C -o BPE
mmdesipio@mmdesipio-Inspiron-3138:~/Documents/Programming/C$ ./BPE

Welcome to this C program!

Please enter your first name here: Matt

Hello, Matt

Please select your option...

1. Evaluate your GPA
2. Skip to the end
3. Evaluate your age
What is your choice?: 4
```

11.3 IF statements

Just like how we did in batch, we are going to create a set of IF
statements to decide what to do with the user's option. An IF
statement in C has the same logic behind it as an IF statement in
BATCH, but the syntax for an IF statement in C is...

If (variable == #/'character') { do this }

So if the user selects choice "1"...

If (choice == 1) {
//choice 1 - evaluate user's GPA
}

We will have a separate IF statement for each of the three choices.
In choice 1, we are going to ask the user for their GPA and store it
as the variable "GPA". Then we will have another series of "nested"
if statements that tells the user what the program thinks of their
GPA. If the GPA is over 4.0 - the program will say that the GPA is
invalid. If the GPA is under 2.0, the program will tell the user to
study. If the GPA is over 2.0, it will congratulate the user.
Disclaimer: no GPA is intended to be labeled as "bad", just a little

program demonstrating IF statements in C. See if you can follow the logic!

```c
printf("\n\nPlease select your option...\n\n");
printf("1. Evaluate your GPA\n");
printf("2. Skip to the end\n");
printf("3. Evaluate your age\n");

printf("What is your choice?: ");
scanf("%d",&CHOICE);

if (CHOICE == 1) {
    //Choice 1 - evaluate the user's GPA
    printf("\nWhat is your GPA?: ");
    scanf("%lf",&GPA);

    if (GPA > 4.0) {
        printf("\nYou have entered an invalid GPA!");
    }
    if (GPA <= 4.0) {
        if (GPA >2.0) {
            printf("\nYou have a great GPA!\n");
        }
        if (GPA <= 2.0){
            printf("\nGet to studying!\n");
        }
    }
}

//End of program
}
```

The program output will look like...

```
Welcome to this C program!

Please enter your first name here: Matt

Hello, Matt

Please select your option...

1. Evaluate your GPA
2. Skip to the end
3. Evaluate your age
What is your choice?: 1

What is your GPA?: 2.8

You have a great GPA!
```

You will notice that "%lf" was used to store the variable as a double. Now let's go back into our code and display what the user entered. If you only wanted to print to 2 decimal points, you could type *%.2lf* instead. See the next image for the code – but it follows the format given earlier.

Choice 2, is fairly easy, we will just have an empty IF statement...

If (choice == 2){
//choice 2 - do nothing - skip to end
}

```c
if (CHOICE == 1) {
   //Choice 1 - evaluate the user's GPA
   printf("\nWhat is your GPA?: ");
   scanf("%lf",&GPA);

   if (GPA > 4.0) {
      printf("\nYou have entered an invalid GPA!");
   }
   if (GPA <= 4.0) {
      if (GPA >2.0) {
         printf("\nYou have a great GPA!\n");
      }
      if (GPA <= 2.0){
         printf("\nGet to studying!\n");
      }
   }
   printf("You have a %.2lf GPA\n",GPA);
}

if (CHOICE == 2) {
   //Choice 2 - Nothing happens
}

//End of program
}
```

Choice 3, is very similar to choice 1, but since we are learning C, let's make it a little more complicated.

11.4 Do-While loop

We will first have to ask the user for their AGE and store it as an integer ("%d"). After this, we can do another series of IF statements. This time, however, we want to introduce the DO-WHILE loop. The DO-WHILE loop, is a loop that commands "Do this, while this is true" - hence its name. The structure is:

Do{
Commands;
}while(condition);

For example, if our loops looks like…

Do{
Commands;
}while(AGE>200);

The program will continue to cycle through the DO-WHILE loop until age becomes less than 200. Once the loop is entered, if the user enters a value for AGE that is less than 200, it will escape the loop. Inside the DO-WHILE loop, we will have our series of IF statements. See if you can follow the logic. Practice this by walking through the loop with different values of AGE.

```c
if (CHOICE == 2) {
   //Choice 2 - Nothing happens
}

if (CHOICE == 3) {
   do{
      printf("\nPlease enter your age here: ");
      scanf("%d",&AGE);
   }while(AGE>200);

   if (AGE <= 50) {
      printf("\nYou are a baby!\n");
   }
   if (AGE > 50) {
      printf("\nYou are an older baby\n");
   }
}

//End of program
}
```

Now our program is functional, but let's implement one more useful tool in C. Let's learn how to check to see if the user entered a valid choice from the menu. Right now, we simply scan in the user entered choice in without checking it. Say for example the user entered "5", what would the program do?

To check this, we use another do while loop. You may have noticed that for C programming, "=" means equal to, ">" means greater than, "<" means less than, "<=" means less than or equal to, and

">=" means greater than or equal to. But what may be less obvious is that "!=" means not equal too. This will prove to be useful in our next code.

Do{

printf("What is your choice?: ");
scanf("%d",&choice);

if(choice != 1 && choice !=2 && choice !=3){
printf("\nYou entered an invalid entry - Please try again\n");
}

}while (choice != 1 && choice !=2 && choice !=3);

Replacing the old code with this code, will improve our program. Now if the user enters an invalid choice, the program will alert them and allow them to type another choice. Now only a 1, 2, or 3 will allow the user to continue with the program.

See the completed program below. Notice the added feature that recalls two variables in the same sentence. We have only touched on the very basics of what C programming is, but you still have earned a solid foundation in it.

11.5 The completed program

```c
// INCLUDES SECTION
#include <stdio.h>
#include <stdlib.h>
#include <ctype.h>
#include <math.h>

// DEFINES SECTION
#define N 64
#define PI acos(-1.0)

// Program main
void main(void) {
  // Variable declarations
  char fname[N];
  int AGE, CHOICE;
  double GPA;

  printf("\nWelcome to this C program!\n\n");

  //Storing a user answered question as a word
  printf("Please enter your first name here: ");
  fflush(stdin);
  scanf("%s",&fname[0]);

  printf("\nHello, %s",&fname[0]);

  printf("\n\nPlease select your option...\n\n");
  printf("1. Evaluate your GPA\n");
  printf("2. Skip to the end\n");
  printf("3. Evaluate your age\n");

do{

  printf("What is your choice?: ");
  scanf("%d",&CHOICE);

  if(CHOICE != 1 && CHOICE !=2 && CHOICE !=3) {
    printf("\nYou entered an invalid entry - Please try again\n");
  }

}while (CHOICE != 1 && CHOICE !=2 && CHOICE !=3);
```

```c
  if (CHOICE == 1) {
    //Choice 1 - evaluate the user's GPA
    printf("\nWhat is your GPA?: ");
    scanf("%lf",&GPA);

    if (GPA > 4.0) {
      printf("\nYou have entered an invalid GPA!");
    }
    if (GPA <= 4.0) {
      if (GPA >2.0) {
        printf("\nYou have a great GPA!\n");
      }
      if (GPA <= 2.0){
        printf("\nGet to studying!\n");
      }
    }
    printf("You have a %.2lf GPA\n",GPA);
  }

  if (CHOICE == 2) {
    //Choice 2 - Nothing happens
  }

  if (CHOICE == 3) {
    do{
      printf("\nPlease enter your age here: ");
      scanf("%d",&AGE);
    }while(AGE>200);

    if (AGE <= 50) {
      printf("\nYou are a baby!\n");
    }
    if (AGE > 50) {
      printf("\nYou are an older baby\n");
    }

    printf("Wow, %s, I would have never guessed you were %d years old!\n",&fname[0],AGE);

  }

//End of program
}
```

Part 4 - G and M code for CNC milling

Chapter 12: G and M code

G and M code can be used to tell a CNC milling machine what to do. A CNC milling machine takes a piece of material and cuts it according to the entered program. Note that there are many ways to communicate with a CNC machine, this is just an interesting practical application of general coding skills.

A G and M code program is essentially a list of commands that the CNC machine recognizes and can complete. The windows command prompt recognizes the command "ECHO" and outputs the text after it, just like how a CNC machine recognizes G00 and moves rapidly to the desired location that immediately follows it. G and M code is similar to BATCH programming in this sense.

When you write code for a CNC machine, you are probably writing the code for the movement of the cutting tool. Say we are cutting a metal cube, a list of G and M codes can be used to control the cutting tool and "cut out" the desired shape. That's all a program with G and M code usually is. Just a list of G and M commands. Often, these programs contain IF statements and FOR loops (the same ones we have seen) - but we will not discuss that any further.

Say you already have your tool set up and your block mounted to the cutting stage. Usually the first thing that has to get done is to find a "zero" on your part. Once you call a point on your block the origin, you can run a program full of G and M code. Usually the process of setting the origin (the zero for the X, Y, and Z axis) is very application/machine specific, so there is no need to cover it here.

Let's assume that you have set the origin (x=0, y=0, and z=0), to the bottom left corner of an aluminum cube.

To start a program in G and M code, we need a **%**. After that, we need to name the program with **o00123**. If you were to write another program later, you could name it "o00124". A comment line in G and M code starts with "/" and every line in G and M code must end with a semicolon. So we see, while G and M code is read in a way similar to BATCH (a list of commands), its syntax also resembles C in this case (semicolons at the end of the line). In G and M, we have to name each "block" of code (line of code). We do this by adding an "N#" before every line of code. It is good practice to do intervals of 5, just in case you have to go back in at a later date and add blocks of new code. It is certainly better to do intervals of 5, then to do intervals of 1 and have to change 1000 names of lines of code later if you insert another line.

So right now, we might imagine our code to look like...

%
O00123
/cutting a block of aluminum
N5 / First line of Code
N10 / Second line of Code
/End of Program
%

Our first block of code is usually our safety line. I will assume you are reading this section of the book out of curiosity. In such a case - you do not need to fully understand the safety line unless you are actually going to be running some CNC programs. If you are, you should consult a better source. However, our safety line will consist of the following commands.

G90 - puts us in absolute coordinates.
G20 - puts our units in inches.
G54 - work offset.
G28 - machine home.
G40 - cancels cutter compensation.
G80 - cancels canned cycle.

All of these commands will be in our N5 block, or our safety line. Our program will take our block of aluminum and smooth out the corners (we will only be cutting a ¼" deep). This will be a basic program, but you will learn a lot about G and M code in the process. Our program looks like...

```
%
O000123
/ Smoothing out the sharp edges of an aluminum block
/ Safety line
N5 G90 G20 G54 G28 G40 G80;
/End of Program
%
```

First thing we now have to do is change our cutting tool. M06 is used to change the tool. T01 is tool #1. So when we use T01 M06, we change the tool to tool #1. Next we have to input the compensation for the tool - G43 is tool length compensation and H01 is the tool offset for tool #1. Next we have to turn on our cutting tool and spin the spindle. M03 is used to turn the spindle clockwise and S2000 turns the spindle at 2000 rpm. Our code now looks like...

```
%
O000123
/ Smoothing out the sharp edges of an aluminum block
/ Safety line
N5 G90 G20 G54 G28 G40 G80;
/ Changing to tool #1
N10 T01 M06;
/ Tool compensation
N15 G43 H01l;
/ Spinning the spindle
N20 S2000 M03;
/End of Program
%
```

Unfortunately, we have only covered the basics here. Now G and M code gets a little tricky - we need to have a very good sense of the coordinates the tool is using. We are in units of inches and we have our zero - the bottom left corner of the piece. Remember we skipped the process of actually zeroing our part. Let's say that our block of aluminum is 4"x4". Let's assume our tool is currently at (x=0, y=0, z=10) - that is, 10 inches directly above the top of our origin. We want to smooth out the sharp corners of our block and make them smooth. We do not want to cut the actual sides of the piece, just the corners (yes, we will be dealing with arcs). Below is a diagram of what we want to do.

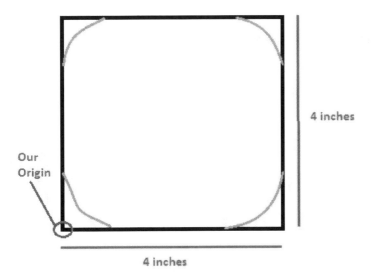

We can imagine a graph under and around our aluminum block. We can see how the bottom left corner of our piece is (0,0,0) - that is (x=0,y=0,z=0). We can imagine that if we go directly horizontal to the right all the way to the bottom right corner of our block that our location would now be (+4,0,0) or simply just (4,0,0), since our piece is 4"x4". We can imagine that if Z is changed to 10, that we wouldn't see a difference from this bird's eye view. We can imagine that if we moved directly vertically from (4,0,0) to the top right corner, that our location would be (4,4,0). Again, (4,4,0) and

(4,4,10) would look identical from this bird's eye view since the Z axis just deals with how close to the top of the piece we are.

Let's say we first want to cut the top left corner, then move clockwise until our last cut is the bottom left corner. We now have to move our cutting tool (remember it is at (0,0,10) right now). To move the cutting tool fast (when not cutting the piece), we use G00. We do not want to cut anything yet, just get our tool in a better spot. We should move our tool to (-0.25,-1.0,10). Moving our tool to the left ¼" inch (x=-0.25), should put the outer edge of our cutting tool's diameter right at the edge of the piece - if we used a ½" diameter bit. Moving our tool to the Y=-1.0 position just moves our tool under our piece by an inch. When the program runs into that block of code (N25), it will move the tool to this location. We need to start N25 with G00, but we do not have to use it in other lines directly after it if we plan to just move our tool with the same G00 setting. Say now, we want to move our Y to -0.5. N30 could simply be Y-0.5 - no "G00" needed. Next we would want to move our piece to Z=1.0 and then Z=-0.25. At Z=-0.25, our tool is below the surface of the aluminum block and will cut the piece when the X and Y are changed so that the bit is over the piece.

Our code now looks like... (These programs get long with comments so I am going to omit them until the end - you should not.)

%
O000123
N5 G90 G20 G54 G28 G40 G80;
N10 T01 M06;
N15 G43 H01l;
N20 S2000 M03;
N25 G00 X-.25 Y-1.0;
N30 Y-.5;
N35 Z1.0;
N40 Z-.25;
/End of Program

%

Now that our tool is set up and in a good location, we can start to cut our piece. N45 will move our cutting tool along the left side of the piece until we hit the point we want to start our curve. Let's say we want to start our curve ½" from the top edge. Notice how N45 uses G01 instead of G00. G01 gives the machine controlled movement and it is necessary to use when cutting the aluminum block. "F15.5" set the feed rate of our cutting tool to 15.5 (whatever the units are).

N45 G01 Y3.5 F15.0;

To give a visual, our tool just did the following movement.

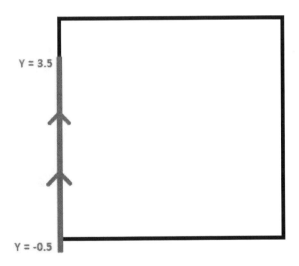

Note that we did not cut anything here, we simply moved along the edge. Maybe we cut some imperfections in the piece along the way, but nothing intentional. Now we need to cut the corner to a smooth curve. Our cutting tool will do this by moving across a defined arc. G02 is used the cut the piece in a clockwise circular motion. The X and Y points that follow are the final X and Y points after the cut is complete. Unfortunately, this information is not enough for the machine, we need to define "I" and "J" as well. Defining I and J can be a little confusing, but it can be easily done by using graph paper. We will instead use some mathematical formulas. "I" is the result of the X arc center point minus the X starting point. "J" is the result of the Y arc center point and Y starting point. This arc center point, is the center of the circle the arc follows. See the next visual.

/start of arc is (-.25,3.5)
/center point of arc is (.5,3.5))
/ I = .5 - -.25 = .75
/ J = 3.5 - 3.5 = 0
N50 G02 X0.5 Y4.25 I0.75 J0.0;

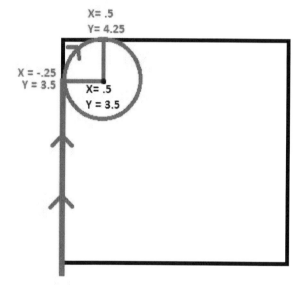

Cutting curves is not necessarily trivial at first, so it may take time getting used to. Our next "cut" will be to move across the top edge of the square until we reach the starting point of our next curve.

N55 G01 X3.5;

Next we have to execute our next curve. This time our end point is (4.25,3.5). Remember we are going ¼" (quarter inch = 0.25 inches) from the edge so that our cutting tool doesn't actually cut anything but is perfectly at the edge of the piece. Using graph paper makes it much easier to figure out what the center point. That being said, if you look at this long enough it becomes fairly easy to figure out. On our next curve, the center point of the arc is (3.5,3.5). What are "I" and "J"?

N60 G02 X4.25 Y3.5 I0.0 J-0.75;

See the visual of our cuts to this point.

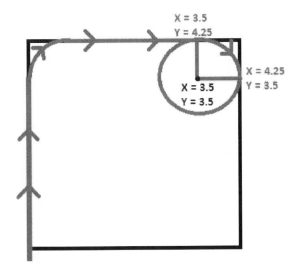

You should now be able to understand the rest of the code. See the visual and comment lines for any help you may need. The complete program is below.

%
O00123

/ Smoothing out the sharp edges of an aluminum block
/ Safety line
N5 G90 G20 G54 G28 G40 G80;

/ Changing to tool #1
N10 T01 M06;

/ Tool compensation
N15 G43 H01l;

/ Spinning the spindle
N20 S2000 M03;

/ Moving the cutting tool to a better position
N25 G00 X-.25 Y-1.0;
N30 Y-.5;
N35 Z1.0;

/ Adjust Z depth according to depth of piece
N40 Z-.25;

/ Moving the piece vertically along the left side
N45 G01 Y3.5 F15.0;

/ Cutting out the top left corner
N50 G02 X0.5 Y4.25 I0.75 J0.0;

/ Moving horizontally along the top
N55 G01 X3.5;

/ Cutting out the top right corner
N60 G02 X4.25 Y3.5 I0.0 J-0.75;

/ Moving vertically along the right side
N65 G01 Y.5;

/ Cutting out the bottom right corner
N70 G02 X3.5 Y-.25 I-.75 J0.0;

/ Moving horizontally along the bottom

N75 G01 X0.5;

/ Cutting out the bottom left corner
N80 G02 X-0.25 Y0.5 I0.0 J0.75;

/ Moving the cutting tool away from the piece
N85 G01 Y5.0;
N90 G00 Z1.0;

/ Stopping the spindle
N95 M05;

/ Sending the machine to the origin - "home"
N100 G28;

/ Ending the program
N105 M30;

/End of Program
%

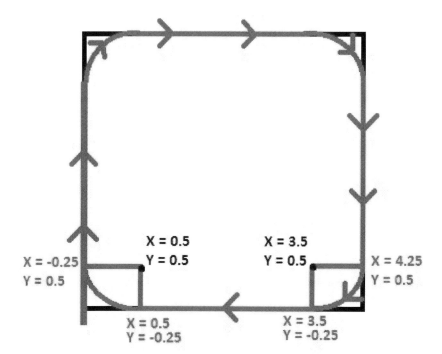

X = -0.25
Y = 0.5

X = 0.5
Y = 0.5

X = 3.5
Y = 0.5

X = 4.25
Y = 0.5

X = 0.5
Y = -0.25

X = 3.5
Y = -0.25

Conclusion

Programming is an interesting skill to learn. We started with basic batch programming to show us the fundamental skills of coding. We moved on to HTML to show a little example of practical programming. C programming showed us that programming languages can be intimidating and complex - but also incredibly useful (and cool). G and M code showed us how some people use basic coding skills every day of their work lives. This text covered each of those languages to show that no matter how different programming languages can be from one another, they all use and require basic fundamental ideas (comments, logic, presentation, etc...) that are great for everyone to learn.

20975525R00054

Printed in Poland
by Amazon Fulfillment
Poland Sp. z o.o., Wrocław